Discover
DRAGONS,
GIANTS,
AND
Other Deadly
Fantasy Monsters

by A.J. Sautter

CAPSTONE PRESS
a capstone imprint

Blazers Books are published by Capstone Press,
1710 Roe Crest Drive, North Mankato, Minnesota 56003
www.mycapstone.com

Library of Congress Cataloging-in-Publication data
Names: Sautter, Aaron, author.
Title: Discover dragons, giants, and other deadly fantasy monsters / by A.J. Sautter.
Description: Mankato, Minnesota : Capstone Press, [2018] | Series: Blazers. all about
   fantasy creatures | Includes bibliographical references and index.
Summary: "In handbook format, describes the physical features, behavior, and
   habitat of deadly fantasy monsters"—Provided by publisher.
Identifiers: LCCN 2017002069 (print) | LCCN 2017014758 (ebook) |
   ISBN 9781515768562 (eBook PDF) | ISBN 9781515768395 (library binding) |
   ISBN 9781515768432 (paperback)
Subjects: LCSH: Animals, Mythical—Juvenile literature. | Monsters—Juvenile literature.
Classification: LCC GR825 (ebook) | LCC GR825 .S275 2018 (print) |
   DDC 398/.45—dc23
LC record available at https://lccn.loc.gov/2017002069

Editorial Credits
Bobbie Nuytten, designer; Wanda Winch, media researcher;
Laura Manthe, production specialist

Photo Credits
Capstone: Colin Ashcroft, 21, 32, Collin Howard, 7, 9, Jason Juta, 4, 15, 27, Martin
Bustamante, cover (bottom left), 1 (left), 5, 17, Stefano Azzalin, 23, Tom McGrath, cover
(top right), 11, 13, 19; Dreamstime: Chorazin3d, 28 (bottom); Shutterstock: BergelmLicht,
cover (background), 1 (background), Firstear, 25, Marafona, 9 (background), Valentyna
Chukhlyebova, 3, 28 (top)

Printed in the United States of America.
010364F17

TABLE OF CONTENTS

DEADLY FANTASY MONSTERS!

Fantasy tales are full of deadly monsters. Dragons
attack villages to steal treasure. Giants, ogres,
and trolls like to **ambush** unwitting travelers.
What would these monsters do if they were real?
Where would they live? What would they eat?
Turn the page and find out!

ambush—to make
a surprise attack

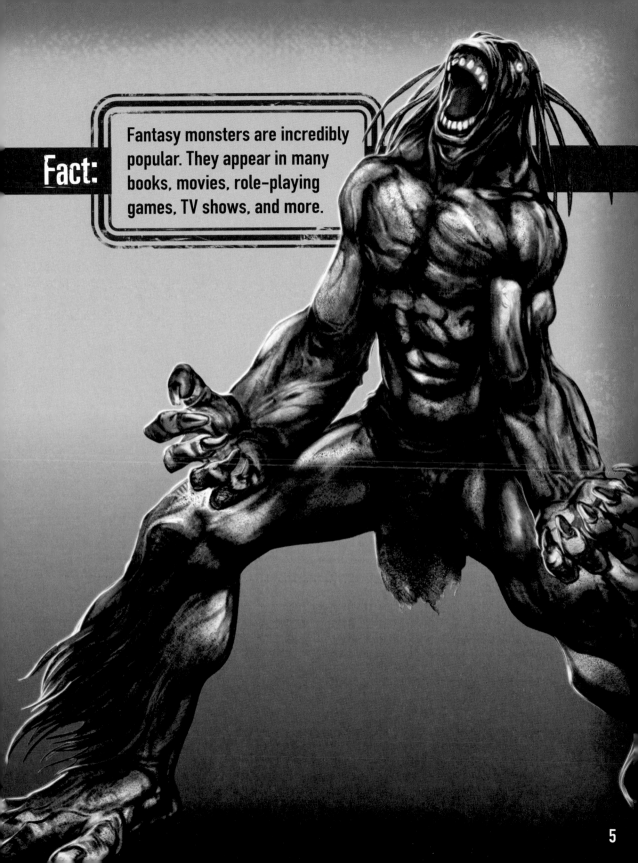

Fantasy monsters are incredibly popular. They appear in many books, movies, role-playing games, TV shows, and more.

BLACK DRAGONS

Size: 120 feet (37 meters) long
wingspans up to 150 feet (46 m)

Home: caves with hidden entrances found
in **bogs** or swamps

Diet: turtles, alligators, opossums, muskrats, humans

Lifespan: up to 2,200 years

Appearance: Black dragons have thin, bony bodies. They often have diseased skin and tattered wings. Like most dragons, black dragons have deadly teeth, claws, and tails. They also have deadly acid breath that can dissolve the thickest armor.

bog—an area of wet, spongy land, often filled with dead and rotting plants

Behavior: Black dragons are vicious and cruel. They enjoy causing pain in others. They also like to collect treasure. They like gold coins more than gems or other valuables.

Eastern Dragons

Size: more than 200 feet (61 m) long
Home: caves found near rivers and lakes
Diet: fish, deer, sheep, rabbits, squirrels
Lifespan: more than 8,000 years

Appearance: Eastern dragons are brightly colored with red, yellow, bluc, or green scales. Their bodies are similar to huge snakes. Most have antlers like a deer. Their four feet are tipped with sharp **talons**. Eastern dragons don't have wings. But they can use magic to soar through the air.

talon—a long, sharp claw
drought—a long period of weather with little or no rainfall

Behavior: Eastern dragons can be deadly, but they are often helpful toward humans. Some have used magic to bring rain and end **droughts**. Eastern dragons enjoy collecting gems like rubies and emeralds.

Red Dragons

Size: 150 feet (46 m) long
wingspans up to 180 feet (55 m)

Home: lairs found in deep caves in large mountains

Diet: deer, sheep, cattle, humans

Lifespan: more than 2,500 years

Appearance: Red dragons usually have dark red or red-gold scales. They have four legs and huge leathery wings. Their weapons include razor-sharp claws, wicked teeth, and powerful whiplike tails.

lair—a place where a wild animal lives and sleeps

hoard—money, gold, or other valuables that are stored or hidden away

Behavior: Red dragons gain their treasure by stealing it. They fiercely protect their treasure **hoards**. If someone tries to steal a single coin, they'll blast the person with their fiery breath.

WHITE DRAGONS

Size: 100 feet (31 m) long
wingspans up to 120 feet (37 m)

Home: icy caves on tall mountain peaks or large icebergs

Diet: fish, walruses, elk, small whales

Lifespan: up to 2,000 years

Appearance: White dragons have white or light blue scales. A bony **frill** helps protect their necks. They have two legs, two large wings, sharp claws and teeth, and powerful tails.

frill—a bony collar that fans out around an animal's neck

grudge—a feeling of anger toward someone who has hurt or insulted you in the past

Behavior: White dragons love treasure, but they like diamonds and silver coins best. They use their icy breath for defense and hunting prey. Ice dragons have long memories. If insulted, they'll hold onto a **grudge** for hundreds of years.

Cyclopes

Size: about 15 feet (4.6 m) tall

Home: mountain caves or ruined castles

Diet: sheep, goats, deer, rabbits, squirrels

Lifespan: 450 to 500 years

Appearance: Cyclopes have stocky bodies and strong hands. Most don't have hair, but a few have bushy beards. Cyclopes are best known for their single large eye. Looking into a Cyclops' eye can cause paralyzing fear in a person.

blacksmith—someone who makes and fixes things made of iron or steel

forge—a special furnace in which metal is heated

Behavior: Most Cyclopes live alone. They spend their days protecting their animals and homes from intruders. Some are skilled **blacksmiths**. They create magical weapons and armor in their secret **forges**.

ETTINS

Size: 20 to 25 feet (6 to 7.6 m) tall

Home: underground caves found in rocky hills

Diet: deer, elk, sheep, goats, humans

Lifespan: 90 to 100 years

Appearance: Ettins have muscular bodies and two or more heads. Each head controls a different part of the body. Ettins never bathe. They usually stink of sweat and rotting food.

Behavior: Ettins will eat any meat they can catch, including humans. They live alone and don't like to be disturbed. Ettins aren't very smart. But they are skilled fighters with their spiked clubs.

Mountain Giants

Size: more than 45 feet (13 m) tall
Home: large caves in mountains or hidden valleys
Diet: deer, elk, sheep, goats, humans
Lifespan: 600 to 700 years

Appearance: Mountain giants look like huge human beings. However, their tough skin is usually a stony gray color. They have black, brown, or fiery red hair. Most males have huge, bushy beards.

Behavior: Mountain giants like to be left alone. If disturbed, they will smash outsiders with their huge clubs. Mountain giants often enjoy rock battles. They hurl huge boulders at one another high up in the mountains.

OGRES

Size: 8 to 10 feet (2.4 to 3 m) tall

Home: damp caves near mountains or stinking swamps

Diet: snakes, snails, slugs, grubs, humans

Lifespan: about 50 years

Appearance: Ogres are amazingly strong. Their tough skin is often green in color. Many ogres have **deformities** such as club hands or hunched backs. Some have sharp tusks in their bottom jaws.

deformity—being twisted, bent, or disfigured in some way

raid—a sudden, surprise attack on a place

Behavior: Ogres hate the sun and avoid sunlight whenever possible. Ogres are usually violent and cruel. They enjoy hurting their enemies and hearing them cry out in pain. Ogres have few skills. They often **raid** nearby villages to steal what they need.

Cave Trolls

Size: 10 to 12 feet (3 to 3.7 m) tall
Home: deep, dark mountain caves
Diet: sheep, deer, horses, dwarves, humans
Lifespan: 65 to 75 years

Appearance: Cave trolls have long arms and huge, muscular bodies. Their rough skin often looks like stone. They have sharp, jagged teeth and two large tusks. They often stand hunched over in an apelike **stance**.

> **stance**—the position of someone's arms, legs, and body

Behavior: Cave trolls are active only at night. If exposed to sunlight, they turn into solid stone. Cave trolls often work with orcs to ambush travelers. Sometimes they steal animals to eat from nearby farms.

FOREST TROLLS

Size: 12 to 15 feet (3.7 to 4.6 m) tall

Home: dark caves hidden in thick forests

Diet: any kind of animal, dwarves, humans

Lifespan: about 200 years

Appearance: Forest trolls have gray or green skin. But their huge bodies are usually covered in thick brown hair. Their mouths are full of jagged, rotten teeth. Large tusks jut out from their lower jaws.

intelligence—the ability to learn and understand information

Behavior: Forest trolls are rarely seen. They will fiercely attack anyone who wanders into their territory. Most trolls have little **intelligence**. But some forest trolls know how to make and use simple armor and weapons.

Swamp Trolls

Size: 8 to 10 feet (2.4 to 3 m) tall
Home: tropical swamps and bogs
Diet: fish, frogs, snakes, muskrats, alligators, humans
Lifespan: 90 to 100 years

Appearance: Swamp trolls have dark green or black skin. Swamp trolls' large hands are tipped with wicked claws. Their mouths are filled with sharp, jagged teeth. Their bodies heal quickly from wounds. Only fire or acid can kill and destroy a swamp troll.

Behavior: Swamp trolls are savage and violent. They attack humans and other creatures on sight. Swamp trolls hate sunlight and are active only at night.

Creature Quiz

1. Ogres raid villages at night to:

    A) steal food and supplies.

    B) avoid sunlight.

    C) both A and B.

2. Red dragons usually live in:

    A) stinking bogs and swamps.

    B) deep caves in the mountains.

    C) large castles or forts.

3. Ettins have more than one head. They usually tend to:

    A) be very intelligent.

    B) be skilled fighters.

    C) argue with themselves.

4. If a cave troll catches you, you should:

    A) try to convince him to let you go.

    B) fight your way past him.

    C) keep him talking until the sun rises.

5. An Eastern dragon's favorite treasure is:

    A) shiny diamonds and silver coins.

    B) colorful jewels and gems.

    C) golden coins.

6. The best weapon to use against a swamp troll is:

   A) fire or acid.

   B) a magic sword.

   C) magic spells and potions.

7. When dealing with a white dragon you should never:

   A) give it food.

   B) insult it.

   C) sing to it.

8. If you meet a Cyclops you should:

   A) buy a weapon from him.

   B) stun him with a magic spell.

   C) never look him in the eye.

9. Black dragons use deadly _____ for defense.

   A) acid breath

   B) fire breath

   C) icy breath

10. If you're in the mountains and rocks begin flying overhead, it could be:

   A) a landslide.

   B) an earthquake.

   C) mountain giants having a rock battle.

See page 31 for quiz answers.

Glossary

ambush (AM-bush)—to make a surprise attack

blacksmith (BLAK-smith)—someone who makes and fixes things made of iron or steel

bog (BAWG)—an area of wet, spongy land, often filled with dead and rotting plants

deformity (di-FORM-ih-tee)—being twisted, bent, or disfigured in some way

drought (DROUT)—a long period of weather with little or no rainfall

forge (FORJ)—a special furnace in which metal is heated

frill (FRIL)—a bony collar that fans out around an animal's neck

grudge (GRUDJ)—a feeling of anger toward someone who has hurt or insulted you in the past

hoard (HORD)—money, gold, or other valuables that are stored or hidden away

intelligence (in-TEL-uh-jenss)—the ability to learn and understand information

lair (LAYR)—a place where a wild animal lives and sleeps

raid (RAYD)—a sudden, surprise attack on a place

stance (STANSS)—the position of someone's arms, legs, and body

talon (TAL-uhn)—a long, sharp claw

Read More

Doeden, Matt. *The Anatomy of a Dragon.* The World of Dragons. North Mankato, Minn.: Capstone Press, 2013.

Forbeck, Matt. *Dungeonology.* Ologies. Somerville, Mass.: Candlewick Press, 2016.

Sautter, A. J. *How to Draw Dragons, Trolls, and Other Dangerous Monsters.* Drawing Fantasy Creatures. North Mankato, Minn.: Capstone Press, 2016.

Quiz Answers:

1:C, 2:B, 3:B, 4:C, 5:B, 6:A, 7:B, 8:C, 9:A, 10:C

Internet Sites

Use FactHound to find Internet sites related to this book.

Visit *www.facthound.com*

Just type in 9781515768395 and go.

 Check out projects, games and lots more at **www.capstonekids.com**

Index